My Advent Calendar Couples' Challenges

Spicing Up the Countdown to Christmas

editions Ava Johnson

WHY PLAY?

Are you looking to add some excitement to your relationship and reconnect with your partner? Our Advent calendar is just what you need! Inside, you'll find 25 challenges designed for adults to enjoy while eagerly anticipating Christmas.

With this booklet, you'll create unforgettable evenings with your partner, whether you're a fresh couple looking to explore or a seasoned duo wanting to reignite the fire in your relationship.

HAVE A BLAST!

HOW TO PLAY?

The rules of the calendar are quite simple!

Every day in December, tear out a page from the Advent calendar and then tackle the challenge with your partner. The challenges get progressively more daring as you approach December 25th.

This is a special game for couples, so always respect your partner.

Please note that we can't be held responsible for any sounds or expressions of pleasure from your partner. Thank you.

IT'S YOUR TURN TO PLAY!

1	2	3	4	5
6	7	8	9	10
11	12	13	14	15
16	17	18	19	20
21	22	23	24	25

ARE YOU UP FOR TODAY'S CHALLENGE?

DECEMBER 1ST

Challenge n°1:
Pen a heartfelt love letter
and present it to your partner.

ADVENT CALENDAR
LOVE CHALLENGES

WARNING: DO NOT PEEK AT THE NEXT CHALLENGE UNTIL TOMORROW.

ARE YOU UP FOR TODAY'S CHALLENGE?

DECEMBER 2ND

Challenge n°2:
Whip up a romantic dinner

(include candles, soothing tunes, and roses).

ARE YOU UP FOR TODAY'S CHALLENGE?

DECEMBER 3RD

Challenge n°3:
Plan a movie night
(pick a romantic flick and snag some popcorn).

ARE YOU UP FOR TODAY'S CHALLENGE?

DECEMBER 4TH

Challenge n°4:
Head out to the countryside for some stargazing
(remember warm attire!).

ADVENT CALENDAR
LOVE CHALLENGES

ARE YOU UP FOR TODAY'S CHALLENGE?

DECEMBER 5TH

Challenge n°5:
Tonight, engage in a board game

(we recommend something for grown-ups!).

ARE YOU UP FOR TODAY'S CHALLENGE?

DECEMBER 6TH

Challenge n°6:
Set up an indoor picnic

(include aphrodisiacal treats).

ARE YOU UP FOR TODAY'S CHALLENGE?

DECEMBER 7TH

Challenge n°7:
Arrange a soothing massage night
(complete with oils, candles, and mood music).

ARE YOU UP FOR TODAY'S CHALLENGE?

DECEMBER 8TH

Challenge n°8:
Serve breakfast in bed
(with flowers, fresh fruit, and chocolate).

ARE YOU UP FOR TODAY'S CHALLENGE?

DECEMBER 9TH

Challenge n°9:
Take a bath with your partner
(champagne, candles, and sultry music encouraged).

ARE YOU UP FOR TODAY'S CHALLENGE?

DECEMBER 10TH

Challenge n°10: Fire off 5 SMS messages to your partner

(get creative with your texts).

ARE YOU UP FOR TODAY'S CHALLENGE?

DECEMBER 11TH

Challenge n°11:
Get artsy with your partner

(painting or pottery, for example).

ARE YOU UP FOR TODAY'S CHALLENGE?

DECEMBER 12TH

Challenge n°12:
Mix up some tantalizing cocktails
(and raise a toast to your love.)

WARNING: DO NOT PEEK AT THE NEXT CHALLENGE UNTIL TOMORROW.

ARE YOU UP FOR TODAY'S CHALLENGE?

DECEMBER 13TH

Challenge n°13:
Plan a photoshoot
(prepare alluring outfits).

ARE YOU UP FOR TODAY'S CHALLENGE?

DECEMBER 14TH

Challenge n°14:
Dance the night away in your living room
(consider some bachata moves).

ARE YOU UP FOR TODAY'S CHALLENGE?

DECEMBER 15TH

Challenge n°15:
Hold a cooking showdown for two

(you can wear aprons, but eventually, clothes must go).

WARNING: DO NOT PEEK AT THE NEXT CHALLENGE UNTIL TOMORROW.

ARE YOU UP FOR TODAY'S CHALLENGE?

DECEMBER 16TH

Challenge n°16:
Pen love notes and hide them

(your partner will uncover them in the coming days).

ARE YOU UP FOR TODAY'S CHALLENGE?

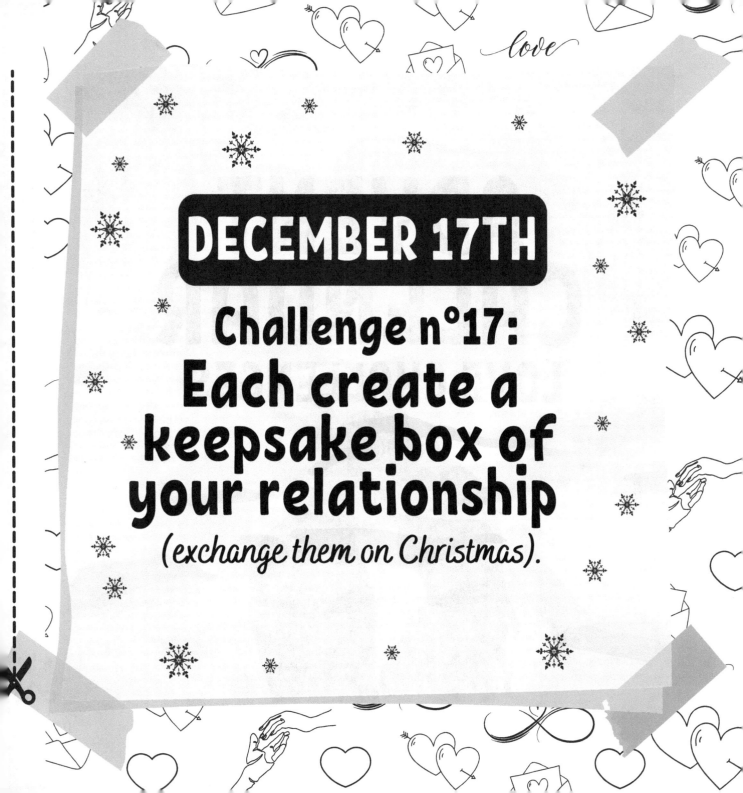

DECEMBER 17TH

Challenge n°17:
Each create a keepsake box of your relationship

(exchange them on Christmas).

ARE YOU UP FOR TODAY'S CHALLENGE?

DECEMBER 18TH

Challenge n°18:
Read a book together

(pick one that'll turn up the heat).

WARNING: DO NOT PEEK AT THE NEXT CHALLENGE UNTIL TOMORROW.

ARE YOU UP FOR TODAY'S CHALLENGE?

DECEMBER 19TH

Challenge n°19:
Try your hand at role-playing
(think firefighter and nurse, for instance).

ARE YOU UP FOR TODAY'S CHALLENGE?

DECEMBER 20TH

Challenge n°20:
Craft a scenario for your first meeting

(seduce your partner like it's the very first time).

ARE YOU UP FOR TODAY'S CHALLENGE?

DECEMBER 21ST

Challenge n°21:
Make a video together

(an adult-themed video, of course).

ARE YOU UP FOR TODAY'S CHALLENGE?

DECEMBER 22ND

Challenge n°22:
Lock lips for a full 120 seconds

(don't be shy about using some tongue!).

WARNING: DO NOT PEEK AT THE NEXT CHALLENGE UNTIL TOMORROW.

ARE YOU UP FOR TODAY'S CHALLENGE?

DECEMBER 23RD

Challenge n°23:
Host a clothes-free evening
(carry out your daily routines in the buff).

WARNING: DO NOT PEEK AT THE NEXT CHALLENGE UNTIL TOMORROW.

ARE YOU UP FOR TODAY'S CHALLENGE?

DECEMBER 24TH

Challenge n°24:
Craft a handmade gift

(you can present it tomorrow).

ARE YOU UP FOR TODAY'S CHALLENGE?

DECEMBER 25TH

Challenge n°25:
Say "I love you" to your partner

(and present your gifts).

THANK YOU FOR YOUR PURCHASE
AND
MERRY
CHRISTMAS!

Made in United States
Troutdale, OR
11/20/2023

14767127R00060